MISSION CREEP:

The Five Subtle Shifts That Sabotage Evangelism & Discipleship

LARRY OSBORNE

MISSION CREEP: The Five Subtle Shifts That Sabotage Evangelism & Discipleship

Credits
Cover Design: Andrew Polfer / Kurt Adams
Editor: Lindy Lowry

Endorsements

Mission Creep reminds us that it is still about Christ's mission of making disciples and what happens when we get out of alignment with the mission. The clarity is classic Larry Osborne - complex concepts made profoundly simple. Every church leader will benefit from this quick and potent read. It's a must for church planters!
Steven M. Pike, Director - Church Multiplication Network

Larry has once again provided some great insight and lenses through which we can examine our practices and see if despite our best intentions we're aiming at the wrong bull's-eye. If you are in Christian ministry I would encourage you to pick up this book and consider the subtle shifts that can make all the difference in the fruitfulness of your disciple-making.
Matt Chandler, Lead Pastor - The Village Church
President - Acts 29 Church Planting Network

Larry Osborne is my favorite contrarian. With grace and truth Osborne points out how the church is undermining its own efforts to accomplish the mission of Jesus. With sage wisdom, Larry plays the part of an encouraging antagonist and points to the bulls-eye of the great commission and shows how the church is missing the mark. *Mission Creep* is a quick read that could make a worldwide impact!
Dave Ferguson, Lead Pastor - Community Christian Church
Spiritual Entrepreneur - NewThing

Larry Osborne hits the bull's-eye in realigning the church with the message and mission of Jesus. I highly recommend it for any church planter, pastor, or church leader.
Dave Page, Director of Church Planting - EFCA West

Osborne clearly identifies five significant but subtle shifts that have taken our churches off course and then shows how to get back on course with the "Mission of God." If you are a church leader, put *Mission Creep* at the top of your reading list
Dr. J. Melvyn Ming, Director of Pastoral Care & Development - Northwest Ministry Network

There is no greater need in the church today than a robust return to the great commission. We are called to make disciples of all nations. The clarity and practical help in *Mission Creep* will transform your church. Read and heed his words.
Darrin Patrick, Lead Pastor - The Journey Church
Vice President - Acts 29 Church Planting Network

Every church starts with a Biblical Mission. Many, if not most, drift away from it. This book highlights the greatest evangelistic challenge in our churches. Every Pastor should take their team through this!
Shawn Lovejoy, Lead Pastor - Mountain Lake Church
Directional Leader - churchplanters.com

Larry, as usual, challenges us to ponder important concepts we would not normally consider. It is always worth wrestling with a wise man's thoughts.
John Worcester, Church Planting Specialist - CNBC

In *Mission Creep*, Larry Osborne is brilliant and simple. He paints a concise picture of what it looks like when the church loses her way. More important he gives a practical path for rediscovering our way back to missional impact. If you are planting or leading a church this book will quickly become your playbook.
David Putman, Lead Navigator - Auxano
Author, Detox for the Overly Religious

Once again Larry has hit it out of the park. This book is a must read for anyone involved in leading or planting churches. It's unquestionably my best read of the year. And I've read all his books – twice. Buy fifty and pass them out to all your friends.
Carolyn Osborne, Larry's Mom

Acknowledgments

I want to acknowledge and thank Todd Wilson, Dave Ferguson, and the entire Exponential team for all they do to advance the Great Commission through recruiting, resourcing, and training church planters.

A special thanks also goes to my administrative assistant, Erica Brandt, and to my wife, Nancy, for their careful editing and helpful critiques. Also, thanks to Lindy Lowry for providing final editorial oversight.

Andrew Polfer and Kurt Adams designed the cover. You guys rock. Thanks for jumping in with such enthusiasm.

The congregation, board, and staff at North Coast Church live this stuff out. They deserve credit for being the lab that proves it works in real-life ministry. My fellow senior pastors here at North Coast, Chris Brown, Charlie Bradshaw and Paul Savona keep it real—and focused— and make ministry fun.

Thanks to Chris Mavity and North Coast Training Network team for providing the training, coaching and consulting that helps church leaders and pastors put these things into practice. You have leveraged well the things God has taught us.

Finally, to my friends at Church Community Builder and Auxano, an enormous thanks for making this book possible. You both provide great tools that help churches see the target and stay on target. Your spiritual fruit grows on other people's trees, but it is incredibly plentiful.

TABLE OF CONTENTS

Chapter One
MISSION CREEP
Why Little Things Matter

On May 10, 1869, crews from the Central Pacific and Union Pacific railroads converged at Promontory Summit in northwest Utah. Their purpose was to connect their two railroads into the first transcontinental railroad.

Starting from the east and west, they had successfully navigated their way across the country to an agreed upon meeting point where they would drive the final *golden spike* into the ground, effectively reducing coast-to-coast travel from an arduous six months to a mere week. It was a phenomenal feat of engineering that had taken six years to complete.

You might think the key to their success was skilled engineering, cartography, and a detailed blueprint. But you'd be wrong.

They certainly had incredibly skilled engineering. They had the best maps available. But the real key to their success was something else. It was their ability to constantly make mid-course corrections.

There was no way they could follow a detailed route. The maps of that day were too primitive. Confronted with a constant barrage of unforeseen obstacles, tunneling challenges, unstable soil, and harsh weather, they had to constantly change their plans in light of their realities and their mission.

Their success wasn't due to the clarity of their plan; it was due to the clarity of their mission. Everyone on both teams knew where they were headed. They knew that no matter what, they had to meet up at some future point with their rails perfectly aligned. Otherwise, all of their hard work, tunnels, bridges, and miles of rail would be for naught.

Ministry is not all that different. We too have a mission—to reach the lost and mature the saints for the glory of God. And like the crews that built that first transcontinental railroad, we also face a constant barrage of obstacles and unforeseen challenges that can easily push us off course.

If we're willing to constantly readjust our methods, priorities, and programs to align with the mission, we'll hit the mark. But if we stubbornly stick to yesterday's route, we'll end up laying lots of tracks without ever getting where we want to go.

Just One Degree

It doesn't take much to get off course. Even a mere one-degree variance makes a huge difference. That's why it's so important that we maintain a ruthless focus and devotion to our primary mission (and a willingness to do whatever it takes to realign with it), or it won't be long until we're headed off in the wrong direction without even knowing it.

Imagine you're assigned to stripe the sideline of the local high school football field for the big game. If you're out of whack by just one degree, you'll be out of alignment by over five feet by the time you get to the far end zone. Even if you're just .01 degree off, you'd still be out of alignment by half a foot or more. That might not seem like much. But on a close play at the pylon, it would be a game changer.

Now stretch that same subtle shift over a longer distance. A flight from San Francisco to Los Angeles would miss the airport by six miles at a one-degree variance. A seemingly tiny .01-degree mistake would put your plane in the Pacific Ocean, over a half-mile off course.

When it comes to alignment and mission—little things matter.

That's what this book is about.

Jesus gave us a mission. It's crystal clear. It's not the least bit ambiguous. We are to make disciples among all nations, baptizing them and teaching them to obey everything he commanded.[1]

To do that, we have to align (and constantly realign) our churches, our ministries, and ourselves towards the task. Now obviously, that doesn't mean that everyone is supposed to pack up and head overseas. It doesn't mean we're all called to professional ministry. But it does mean that every one of us is called to contribute to the cause. We're all supposed to play our role, use our spiritual gifts, and fulfill our calling so that together we can make his glory known, reaching the lost and discipling the saved.[2]

Mission Creep

Unfortunately, we've had some mission creep. A series of subtle shifts in focus have thrown us off course. And though these shifts are minor and unintended, over a long period of time they add up. We've missed the mark. So much so that many churches report few converts and few disciples growing to full maturity.[3]

Now I want to be clear. I am not saying that we aren't trying to reach the lost and disciple the saints. We are. Most churches and Christians I know genuinely want to fulfill the Great Commission. They work hard at it. They have pure hearts. They have the best of intentions.

But like a pilot trying to fly from San Francisco to LAX with a miscalibrated flight plan, they keep missing the landing strip.

I'm also not saying that we aren't reaching the lost and maturing the saints. We are. People still come to Jesus all the time. They grow to maturity. Jesus promised he'd build his church. He keeps his promises.[4]

But in many cases, we are incredibly inefficient and ineffective. It's as if we're trying to fight the spiritual battle with one hand tied behind our back.

One of the biggest problems we face is simple inertia. Once we've gotten off track by even the smallest degree, we tend to stay off track. It's human nature to keep heading in the same direction, even if it's a wrong direction. It's also a law of physics. No wonder it's so hard to get back on track.

Two things make it particularly hard to stay in alignment.

First, it takes a while to even notice that we've drifted. The smaller and more subtle the shift, the longer it takes for the consequences to show up. If we aren't vigilant about constantly checking our progress against our mission, we can go a long way before anyone notices that something is out of whack.

Second, by the time we do notice that we're no longer on target, many of our programs, patterns, and structures are so well established that it's easier to proclaim a new target than to make a hard turn to the left or right.

We're like an archer who consistently misses the target two feet to the right but doesn't worry because he's happily painted a new bull's-eye exactly where his arrows keep landing. In fact, not only is he happy, he thinks he's an Olympian. After all, he never misses the bull's-eye.

In the following pages we'll look at the bull's-eye God gave us and five subtle shifts that have caused our arrows to land elsewhere.

We'll discover how these subtle shifts have unintentionally sabotaged our best efforts at evangelism and discipleship and what we can do in practical and real-world terms to recalibrate our focus to fully align with the mission of making disciples and teaching them to obey everything Jesus taught.

But first, we have to make sure we fully understand our mission and what it means to hit the target. And to do that, we need three things: clarity, alignment, and agreement as to what success looks like.

Chapter Two
WHAT SUCCESS LOOKS LIKE
Sizing Up the Bull's-Eye

Making disciples and teaching them to obey everything that Jesus taught us can be broken into a three-part process. At the church I serve, North Coast Church, we're constantly asking if these three things are happening—and measuring to see how well we are doing.

We don't want stories. We want names and faces. We want facts.

Here's what we look for and what we measure.

(1) New Followers of Jesus

The first step in the Great Commission is recruiting new Jesus followers. It's what we commonly call evangelism. While a person's response to the gospel is out of our control (it's ultimately the work of the Spirit), Jesus clearly instructed us to winsomely share the gospel.

And when we do, it's reasonable to expect some folks to step over the line and start to follow Jesus. And if they don't, we need to be like the Apostle Paul, willing to adjust our methods and strategies so that some do.[5]

That's why we're committed to keeping careful track of how many people become followers of Jesus through our ministries and messages. We count so-called decisions and then measure our retention rate at 12 months, 18 months, and three years.

We measure both decision and retention because we don't want to confuse good intentions with actually following Jesus. We realize that it's one thing to make a nod to God or to have a temporary desire to start following Jesus. It's another thing to actually get in line and start following him.[6]

Now I want to be clear. We're not attempting to raise the "following-Jesus" bar so high that only a select few spiritual Navy SEALs are considered as genuine Christ followers. From our vantage point, the very last person in the following-Jesus line is still a Jesus follower. But at the same time, we don't want to fool ourselves into thinking that we are successfully recruiting Jesus followers when all we really did was bring them to the point of good intentions. Those who want or claim to follow Jesus but never give any evidence of following cannot be claimed as recruits. On this the Bible is quite clear.[7]

(2) New Christians Learning to Live the Christian Life

The second step in the Great Commission is training newly baptized believers to obey everything that Jesus taught. Now admittedly that's a hard task, and still harder to measure. But it's not impossible.

To measure if new believers (and longtime believers) are learning to live the Christian life, we have to measure the right things. But too often we've measured the wrong things: intellectual knowledge, doctrine, and spiritual disciplines.

The best way to measure spiritual growth is to look for sin, not righteousness. When lots of sin breaks out, you know that your people aren't learning to obey everything Jesus taught. It's time to change course. It's time to rebuke and instruct more carefully.

But the absence of outward sin (or the presence of good doctrine and spiritual disciplines) is not in itself proof that your people are growing in Christ and learning to obey what he taught.

Let me explain.

Measuring spiritual health is a lot like measuring physical health. My wife had cancer years ago. To this day, no doctor can say with certainty that she is cancer free. All they can say is that there is no detectable cancer.

Even the most thorough and positive checkup doesn't guarantee that we have good health. Cancer and other disease can be spreading unnoticed. It's the same with sin. The standard outward measures of righteousness can easily hide pride, lust, and a host of other pernicious sins.

That's why at North Coast we've taken the route that a doctor takes. We look for signs of sin. In the absence of sin, we *assume* health until something tells us differently. And in the presence of sin, we know exactly what things we need to be teaching them to obey.

(3) Every Christian With an Identifiable Ministry

The final step in discipleship is releasing a disciple into ministry. I don't mean to imply that finding our calling and gift is an upper-division course. From day one, we all have a calling and a gift.

I'm simply acknowledging that until someone knows what God has called and gifted him or her to do (and they are released to do it), we haven't finished the task. They've not yet been taught to obey everything Jesus taught us.

To see how we are doing in this, we periodically measure the percentage of our congregation who have an identifiable area of ministry. It doesn't have to be in our church setting. All we ask is that they are serving somewhere to advance the kingdom—and that they understand what they are doing is a spiritual assignment from God aligned with their passion, giftedness, and calling.

Once again, this is pretty easy to measure. At our last count, well over 70 percent of our congregation had an identifiable ministry connected to our church or one of our community service partners. By measuring this, along with the other two parts of the Great Commission task, we can know where we are, what we need to work on, and how close we are to hitting the bull's-eye.

Without these measurements, there would be no way to tell. You'll have to figure out your own measurements. I offer these by way of description, not prescription. But if we don't label the target and then measure how close we are to hitting it, we're likely to end up self-deceived, painting a new target wherever our arrows land.

Chapter Three
WHAT'S GONE WRONG?
How Contagious Christianity Became a Repulsive Religion

God expects us to be spiritually contagious.

He desires that those who hang around us will see our good deeds and glorify him on the day he visits.[8] Yet, too often today, the world that hangs around us seems to see something else. And what they see doesn't draw them. It repels them.

Those who love the darkness will always reject and ridicule those who bring the light. It's nothing new. It shouldn't surprise us when we are rejected or persecuted. It happened to Jesus. It happened to the early church.[9] It will happen to us.

But at the same time, as Jesus and the early church were being persecuted they were also drawing people to themselves. They were contagious, so much so that the early church exploded with growth despite fierce Roman, Jewish, and Satanic opposition.

So what's happened today?

Why does the Western church see the persecution and rejection without the corresponding contagious attraction and growth? How is it that we've become either irrelevant (a quaint historical preservation society) or repulsive (a narrow-minded and intolerant slice of society) in the eyes of our peers?

To understand what's gone wrong and what we can do to fix it, it's helpful to compare evangelism and discipleship in the church today with what God originally intended. We're supposed to be a church where three things happen: (1) Evangelism is natural, (2) People are changed, and (3) Our communities are made better.

Let's look at each one of these traits more closely to see what's gone wrong.

Evangelism Is Supposed to Be Natural—Not Contrived

When all is well, evangelism happens naturally. Whether it means articulately sharing Christ directly or simply inviting our lost friends to come and see Christianity in action. When Christ has genuinely been set apart as Lord, people will be drawn to him. They will want to find out more.

Unfortunately, the better we've gotten at producing evangelistic programs and special events, the more we've lost the art of natural conversation and the simple form of come-and-see evangelism that revolves around the timing of God's work in the lives of our lost friends— instead of our church's schedule of special outreach events.

As a result, most modern-day recorded decisions for Christ are the result of some sort of special outreach events. That's not to say that these decisions are not genuine decisions for Christ. Many are. Our special events produce genuine Christians. But trying to reach our world with special outreach events is like trying to populate our earth with artificial insemination.

Artificial insemination produces real babies who are a great blessing to those who otherwise would have no children. These kids grow up into real men and women, blessings to their community. But it's an awful expensive and inefficient way to have children. And it would never work as a plan to fill the earth.

People Are Supposed to Be Changed—Not Merely Touched

I minister in San Diego. It's pretty much a post-Christian culture. There are few, if any, remaining signs of cultural Christianity. Hardly any of my neighbors go to church—even on Easter.

In some ways, that's a good thing. Because around here it's much easier to figure out who is a Christ follower and who isn't. There's no need to pretend to be a Christian if you aren't one. Even better, when presenting the gospel, I run into few people who have been spiritually inoculated.

Let me explain.

One of the best ways to keep someone from getting a disease is to inoculate them with a small dose of the disease. That's exactly what the American church did for decades. Many of our churches confused Christianizing our culture with reaching people for Jesus. They considered it a win to offer prayer before a football game, an invocation at a city council meeting, or to place a manger scene in the city square.

When huge crowds swelled attendance at Easter and Christmas Eve, most of us saw it as a good thing. Even if none of them showed up again until next year, we figured that at least they had a taste of the gospel. When a 1990 Gallup Poll showed a record 74 percent of U.S. adults over 18 claimed to have made a commitment to

Christ, many saw it as a great thing, the possible forefront of a national revival.[10]

It was anything but. In the long run, all we did was inoculate an entire culture. They were touched, but not changed. And now they have just enough of the antibodies to make catching the real disease nearly impossible.

Our Communities Are Supposed to Be Made Better– Not Bitter

For far too long we expected our communities to do something for us instead of us doing something for our communities. As a result, many non-Christian community leaders have come to see us as a leach, expecting special favors, sucking tax dollars, and offering nothing of value to those who don't go to church.

Thankfully, there are many churches that have recently taken a different tack. They've made it their goal to serve their community so well that they'd be sorely missed if they left. Many have done it so well that they've received commendations and awards from both city and government leaders.

Unfortunately, much of the damage has already been done. After decades of taking, many community leaders still have a knee-jerk negative response to our churches, so much so that legal battles to expand or build a church have become commonplace. NIMBY (Not In My Back Yard) seems to be the prevailing attitude of the day.

Once again, we have brought this upon ourselves. We've been salt in the saltshaker. And though many of us are now getting out of the saltshaker and into the community, we have a long way to go until the prevailing attitude becomes, "Did you hear the good news? They're starting up a new church in our community."

Can We Stem the Tide?

All of these things have contributed to an increasingly negative overall view of Christians, churches, and pastors.

While some find hope in recent research that finds increasing numbers of younger adults claiming to like Jesus, but not the church, I find little comfort in it. The reality is that those who make such a claim are seldom *following* Jesus. They merely like the image of Jesus that they've come up with in their mind's-eye.

The local church is God's plan A. There is no plan B. When the church repels (or becomes irrelevant), the ministry of Jesus is thwarted. We are his bride, his body, and his family. When we fail to show his beauty and grace, there is no one to step up and take our place.

Frankly, we've been overrun by a cultural tsunami. The culture wars are over. We lost. But that shouldn't cause us to give up hope. We are in far better shape than the early church was in Rome. The hostilities we face and the cultural opposition are nothing compared to what the early church faced.

Yet I am hopeful. The tide can be stemmed. My hope is not in human efforts. My hope is in Jesus's promise. He said he would build his church, and the gates of hell could not hold it back.[11] I believe that as we take note of our drift and humbly realign our churches and ourselves with our God-given mission and calling, we have every reason to believe that God can and will work powerfully.

So let's look at the Five Subtle Shifts that have sabotaged evangelism and discipleship and what we can do to realign each of them.

Chapter Four
SUBTLE SHIFT #1
From Disciples to Decisions

Every great adventure starts with a decision.

Without a decision, nothing ever gets done.

It's the same in the spiritual realm. The journey of discipleship always begins when someone makes a decision to follow Jesus. Without these decisions for Christ, there would be no followers of Christ. So decisions are important—incredibly important.

Yet getting someone to make a decision for Christ isn't the bull's-eye of evangelism. At least it isn't supposed to be. The bull's-eye is making disciples. That's the target Jesus told us to aim for. Everything else is just part of the process.

Unfortunately, there has been a slow and subtle shift away from making disciples to getting decisions.

It's easy to understand why. Not only is the discipleship bull's-eye hard to hit, it's hard to measure. It takes time to know if someone's good intentions or sincere desire actually translates into following Jesus. On the front end, a nod to God and a life-changing step of faith often look alike. Only time will tell.

On top of that, it's far easier to count decisions. We may still claim that making disciples is our ultimate goal. But in reality, many of us primarily aim at getting people to declare a decision to start following Jesus.

It's what we count.

It's what we celebrate.

So it's what we get.

Now a decision is an important first step in the discipleship process. But when decisions replace making disciples as our measure of Great Commission success, we've started down a road of unintended consequences that will eventually take us far away from what Jesus called us to do.

What's The Difference?

A *decision* reflects my good intentions. It may or may not lead to actually following Jesus.

A *disciple* goes beyond good intentions. He or she actually follows Jesus.

Now don't get me wrong. There is nothing wrong with helping someone make a decision for Christ. Good intentions often lead to great actions. Discipleship always starts with a decision.

But not every good intention is worth celebrating. Many last for only a season. Some are forgotten before the night is over. We've all been there. In fact the physical fitness industry depends upon these types of decisions. If everyone who *decided* to get into shape and paid for a membership showed up, there'd be no room in the gym.

The problem isn't helping people come to a decision to follow Christ. That's a good thing. The problem comes when we equate a decision with a disciple. When we begin to count everyone who expresses a desire to follow Christ, says a prayer, or walks the aisle to be genuine converts, we walk away thinking that we've hit the evangelistic bull's-eye even when very few of those decisions actually produce a disciple.

Now once again, don't get me wrong. I'm not defining a disciple as some sort of super saint. I'm not raising the bar so that only a few get in. As far as I'm concerned, everyone in the following-Jesus line is a genuine disciple.

The Greek word (*mathétés*) simply means a pupil or apprentice. It includes the front of the line and the very last person in line. Some disciples are on fire and deeply committed to Jesus. Some struggle. And some are so frightened and skittish that they hang back like Joseph of Arimathea, a secret disciple who laid low until he shocked everyone by stepping forward to claim Jesus's body.[12]

All of these are disciples. All of these are a win. They've moved beyond the good intentions of a decision to the reality of genuinely following Jesus. And it's these kinds of folks that we've been called to count and celebrate. They represent the evangelistic bull's-eye.

Unfortunately, it took me a while to understand the difference between a decision and a disciple. I came to Christ in an environment that equated evangelism with decisions. It's what we aimed at. It's what we celebrated. So I picked up my Bible and went to work fulfilling what I thought the Great Commission called me to do.

How I Learned The Difference

I have to admit. When I first came to Jesus, I went a little bit overboard. Okay, a lot overboard. Maybe that's why they called me a "Jesus Freak."

The change in my life was so epic that I wanted to tell everyone. So I pretty much did. If we crossed paths, I considered it a divine appointment. In most cases, it wasn't long until I found a way to talk about Jesus.

I helped lead a door-to-door evangelism program in our little Baptist church. Each week we would show up unannounced at the home of visitors and neighbors. We'd knock on their door and ask a few leading questions designed to get us to the two questions we really wanted to ask.

> (1) *"Have you come to the place in your spiritual life where you can say you know for certain that if you were to die today you would go to heaven?"*

> (2) *"Suppose that you were to die today and stand before God and he were to say to you, 'Why should I let you into my heaven?' What would you say?"*

Every week we had people pray with us to receive Christ. Every week. Without fail. Upon returning to the church, we'd share stories and rejoice in the eternal consequences of all the decisions that had been made.

Around that same time, our youth pastor put together something we called The Beach Bus. Once a week, we'd drive our church bus from Whittier to Huntington Beach via the famous Beach Boulevard. We'd put a Christian on each seat and pick up hitchhikers. In exchange for a free trip to the beach, they had to listen to our sales pitch (err, the gospel).

We'd hang out at the beach for a while and then head back home in the late afternoon to pick up more hitchhikers so we could tell them about Jesus. And every week we saw folks make decisions for Christ.

I did much the same at the grocery store I worked at. I was quickly dubbed "preacher boy" because of my passion for sharing the gospel with anyone who would listen. I wore the title as a badge of honor. And I rejoiced each time I "led someone to Christ."

Then a friend asked me a horrible question.

He wanted to know where were all the people I was

supposedly leading to Jesus.

I told him I didn't know or care. What was important was that they'd prayed to receive Christ. It was my job to share the gospel and introduce them to Jesus. It was the Spirit's job to follow up, plug them into a church, and grow them to maturity.

Then he pulled out his Bible and asked me to carefully read the Great Commission.

> Therefore go and make disciples of all nations, baptizing them in the name of the Father and of the Son and of the Holy Spirit, and teaching them to obey everything I have commanded you. And surely I am with you always, to the very end of the age."[13]

"Where," he asked, "do you see Jesus breaking this assignment into two parts? And where do you find him giving you permission to focus solely on getting people to make a 'decision' to start following him?"

I had no answer. So I did what every young, passionate, and arrogant new Christians does. I wrote him off.

But his question haunted me. Later that week I began to look more closely at the fruit of my evangelistic efforts. To my chagrin, I discovered that this "preacher boy" had lots of decisions to point to, but not one disciple.

There was literally no one I could point to in our church (or any church for that matter) who had come to Christ through our door-to-door campaign, our Beach Bus, or my evangelistic efforts at work. Not one. They had all prayed and disappeared. Or to be brutally honest, they'd never shown up in the first place.

That shook me.

I realized that I had changed the bull's-eye so that I could hit it more easily. I'd become an expert at turning spiritual interest and good intentions into a prayer. But I was lousy at turning anyone into a disciple.

I was missing the mark, but celebrating as if I was hitting it with world-class accuracy.

What Did Jesus Say?

I should have known better. After all, Jesus was quite clear that good intentions (and good starts) don't guarantee a happy ending.

The Parable of the Four Soils

One of his best-known teachings is the Parable of the Sower. Found in Matthew 13:1-23, it tells the story of a farmer casting seed onto four types of soil. Some of his seeds land on hardpan soil and are quickly eaten by birds. Some fall on shallow soil where the seeds quickly sprout but just as quickly wither and die under the baking sun because they have no roots. Still, other seeds fall among weed-infested soil. They, too, pop up quickly, but are soon choked out by the weeds. Finally, some of his seed falls on good soil where it germinates and grows to harvest.

Today, some people turn this passage into a launching pad for theological debate, especially in terms of eternal security. But I guarantee you that none of Jesus's original listeners took it that way. As members of an agrarian society, they would have never argued about the relative merits of the different kinds of soil.

To a farmer, any seed that fails to grow to harvest is a tragic waste. No one would be satisfied with quick germination, or even a patch that popped up and temporarily looked good before dying off. For a farmer, the goal is harvest. Anything else misses the target. And nothing short of harvest is worthy of celebration.

By the way, the soil that bears a harvest of 100, 60, or 30 times what was sown is not some sort of super fertile soil. Having grown up in the suburbs, I always thought that was a huge return on investment. But my farming friends laugh at me. That's the normal return per seed. It's the ratio that would be expected at the harvest of almost anything.

The Parable of Two Brothers

Consider also Jesus's story about two brothers who were asked by their father to go and work in his fields.[14]

The first one said, "I will not."

The second one said, "I will, sir."

But at the end of day, it was the one who originally said no that went. And the one who said he would go never showed up.

Jesus then asked, "Which of the two did what his father wanted?"

The obvious answer was the one who had originally said, "No." The brother with the good intentions but no follow-through made the right decision—but failed to take the right actions. And his lack of action rendered his original decision worthless.

Towards Realignment

In both of these parables, Jesus illustrates the difference between merely good intentions and actual discipleship. Good starts and good intentions are no guarantee of a happy ending. And for those who understand the difference, there is no way we can be satisfied with decisions that don't produce disciples.

To realign our evangelistic bull's-eye with the target Jesus originally gave us in the Great Commission, we'll have to make some changes. It's not that we need to stop seeking decisions. Decisions are an important part of the process. If we stop seeking decisions, we'll cease making disciples. But we will need to change two things that are commonplace in our churches and ministries: what we celebrate and what we report.

Let me explain.

What Do We Celebrate?

Every organization gets what it celebrates and rewards. It's a leadership axiom. That's why the little Baptist church I was saved in had so many decisions for Jesus. It's what we celebrated. We were so busy high-fiving and chest-bumping over our successful evangelistic efforts that no one seemed to notice that despite a constant stream of new decisions for Christ, the church hadn't grown for years.

Even more ironic was our Jekyll and Hyde response to the people who made these decisions to follow Jesus. When we were wearing our evangelism hat, we celebrated each decision as proof of salvation (we were big on eternal security). But when we were wearing our Bible study hat, we labeled as counterfeit every so-called Christian who didn't regularly show up at church, abide by all or our extra-biblical rules, or see every doctrine the way we did.

In other words, on Wednesday we would celebrate your eternal salvation. But on Sunday we explained why people like you were going to hell. Yet no one seemed to see the contradiction. We were too busy celebrating our decisions to notice the lack of disciples.

To counter the tendency to celebrate decisions instead of disciples, the church I serve focuses on celebrating stories of life change. Instead of pumping up our congregations with statistics indicating the large number of people who indicate that they've stepped over the line to start following Jesus (and there are many), we pick out stories of those who started following Jesus in the recent past and have given evidence of great life change. Then in videos, email blasts, and inter-staff communications we share those stories.

It keeps our focus and excitement on what matters. It helps us ensure that our evangelistic bull's-eye doesn't drift away from celebrating disciples to celebrating decisions. It keeps our eye on the target Jesus asked us to hit.

What Do We Report?

A close cousin of what we celebrate is what we report.

I've noticed over the years that whatever I publically report, I'm internally driven to increase. I think that's why an early ministry mentor encouraged me not to report the number of decisions for Christ that we were seeing in our church.

He told me to carefully count them, track them, and evaluate them. But he suggested that once I started posting the number in an annual report or any public forum, I would be tempted to start manipulating people to manipulate the numbers.

I think he was right. Once we start posting the numbers of anything, people expect us to maintain or exceed those numbers the next time. And if we don't, it won't be long until some folks are advocating for a change in leadership.

People use what we report as a scorecard. It tells them if we are winning or losing. It's human nature. It doesn't matter if it's the stock price of a publically traded company, the win/loss record of a sports team, or the attendance at First Church. We live in a culture that expects numbers to go up and to the right.

That's why some parachurch ministries that focus on decisions always have more decisions this year than last year. To continue raising money, they have to exceed expectations. No one seems to notice that the numbers don't add up. They report massive numbers of decisions for Christ, yet our churches aren't growing by anything close to that number. And if you go back and compile the numbers over the years, you'd think that everyone on earth has been saved four times over.

Again, at the church I serve, we track decisions. Carefully. But we only report them internally. That's not to say that the number of decisions we see is a state secret. We give it out to anyone who asks. It's just to say that we don't report it or broadcast it to everyone.

Doing so has helped us avoid the drift toward decisions supplanting disciples. It has helped us keep our time, money, and energy focused on hitting the evangelistic bull's-eye that Jesus gave us. It has enabled us to evaluate the ministries and methods we use to gather decisions in light of how many disciples they produce—and it has given us the ability to drop things that produce lots of decisions but few disciples.

I guarantee you. If we'd been reporting decisions on a regular basis, we could have never abandoned any of these high-decision, low-disciple programs or ministries. We would have been too driven to see the decision numbers go up and to the right.

Chapter Five
SUBTLE SHIFT #2
From Obedience to Doctrine

When it comes to evangelism and discipleship, obedience is a big deal. It's not an extra credit item. It's not the gold standard. It's the only standard.

Unfortunately, early on in my faith journey I picked up an opposite message. I thought the telltale sign of a genuine Christian was a deep and accurate knowledge of the Bible and theology.

The churches and ministries I hung around focused on the debatable passages of scripture and doctrinal unity. It's what they taught. It's what they believed. And they questioned the salvation of anyone who claimed to be a Christ follower but failed to line up precisely with their understanding of scripture.

It is no wonder that I thought heaven's entrance exam involved a Scantron instead of a blood test. It's what everyone told me.

Now I want to be clear. Doctrine is important. It's very important. Bad doctrine leads to bad living. What we believe about God, salvation, sanctification, and eternity matters. It has a tremendous impact on the choices we make and how we relate to the world around us.

I'm a Bible guy. Unapologetically. I spend a lot of time teaching biblical doctrine. Sermons at North Coast Church are long and in-depth. We recently spent 62 weeks marching through Luke and 48 weeks in Genesis. We use plain language so that those who have never opened a Bible and don't know God can understand what we are saying (and we have tons of those kinds of folks). But we don't hold anything back.

At the same time, I never want to forget that Jesus didn't command us to make sure that the people we disciple have flawless doctrine. He commanded us to teach them to *obey* everything he taught. The difference is subtle, but significant.

Now obviously people can't obey what they don't know. Like many of you, I've had both non-Christians and believers tell me the goofiest things backed up by a Bible verse taken completely out of context. In fact, it has happened to me so often that I eventually wrote a book titled, *Ten Dumb Things Smart Christians Believe*.[15]

Yet at the end of the day, obedience is more important that doctrine. Unfortunately, it's a lesson many of us have forgotten. It's a lesson I had to learn the hard way.

Three Out of Six

During my first years of walking with Jesus, I was deeply influenced by six key mentors. Some I knew well. A couple I knew mostly through their public ministry. Each had a profound impact on my theology, faith, and approach to ministry. I looked up to them and dreamed of being like them someday. In my mind, they represented the epitome of spiritual maturity.

Two were brilliant scholars who taught directly from the original languages. All the others had powerful Bible-based ministries and a solid grasp of theological nuances. Their biblical fidelity was unquestioned. They seemed to have a Bible verse for every situation and a biblical answer for every question. They stirred in my heart a hunger to know the scriptures.

They were also all hard-driving Type-A personalities, unusually disciplined and well- ordered in their thinking and behavior.

Daily devotions? Check.

Doctrinal purity? Check.

A solid grasp of apologetics? Check

The ability to articulately share their faith? Check.

A biblical worldview? Check.

Self-discipline? Check.

Personal sacrifice? Check.

Yet before the decade was over, three of the six would fail a rather important spiritual test. Despite their incredible grasp of theology and doctrine, despite their mastery of the so-called spiritual disciplines, they couldn't keep their pants on. They failed the test of obedience. Sexual fidelity proved to be too much for them.

Now I'm not here to cast stones. I realize that some of God's best have failed the same test. If Peter could deny Jesus, Abraham lie under pressure, and David could murder a close friend and steal his wife, only God knows the evil I'm capable of.

Yet the moral failure of half my mentors left me shaken. It messed with my paradigm of spiritual maturity. And it taught me an important lesson I've never forgotten: *Godliness is not determined by what we know. It's determined by how we obey.*

Why Obedience Is More Important Than Doctrine

Like many, I had fallen into the trap of equating knowledge and a proper grasp of doctrine with spiritual maturity. I assumed that the more I knew, the better I'd live. So when it came time to disciple people, I focused primarily on making sure that they knew the Bible inside out and got all of our doctrines right. I figured obedience would naturally follow.

I was wrong.

It's the exact opposite. Obedience begets spiritual knowledge. Whereas knowledge may or may not produce obedience. Here's why.

The Dimmer Switch Principle

When we obey the light we have, God gives us more light. When we disobey the light we have, he gives us less light. I call it the *dimmer switch principle.*

In Romans 1:18-32, the Apostle Paul describes what happens when an entire culture rejects general revelation and the knowledge of his presence and power that he has written on the hearts of all mankind. At each step of willful disobedience, God turns down the dimmer switch. He gives them over to greater darkness.

The opposite happens when we walk in righteousness and obedience. Our path grows progressively brighter with each step of obedience. Proverbs 4:18 describes it as being like the rising of the sun from the first glimpse of dawn to the full light of day.

If you're an early riser, you know that it's hard to see much at the crack of dawn. That's because our night vision is like our peripheral vision. It lacks depth perception and color. But as the sun comes up, our day vision takes over. The things we could barely see at dawn are brought into sharp relief.

In other words, it's obedience that produces proper doctrine, not the other way around.

That's why obedience is the ultimate goal of the Great Commission. It's at the core of what it means to know, love, and follow Jesus. Let's see what I mean.

The Great Commission

Jesus didn't tell us to go and make disciples of all nations, teaching them great doctrine. He told us to, "Go and make disciples of all nations . . . teaching them to *obey* everything I have commanded you."[16]

So according to the words of Jesus, the goal of the Great Commission is obedience. It's not scholarship, doctrinal acuity, or a self-feeding Bible scholar. It's an obedient Christian.

There's nothing wrong with producing well-taught, biblically accurate Christians. That's a good thing. As a pastor and Bible teacher, I've spent my life helping people become well-taught and biblically accurate. But it's not *the* thing. It's not the bull's-eye. Obedience is.

Knowing God

In the same vein, the ultimate proof that we genuinely know God is not found in what we know about God. It's found in how well we obey God. The Apostle John put it this way:

> We know that we have come to know him if we obey his commands. The man who says, "I know him but does not do what he says is a liar, and the truth is not in him. But if anyone obeys his word, God's love is truly made complete in him. This is how we know we are in him.[17]

Loving God

It's the same for loving God. Jesus said the irrefutable proof that we love him is found in our obedience to him: "If you love me, you will *obey* what I command."[18]

It's not found in the intensity of my intellectual

pursuit or my hard-earned ability to parse every word of scripture. It's found in my obedience.

When Doctrine Trumps Obedience

Once again, I am not denigrating the value of biblical knowledge. I'm not anti-doctrine. I'm pro-obedience.

The Bible is our only infallible source of teaching, rebuking, correcting, and training in righteousness.[19] It tells us who our God is, what he's done, and how he wants us to live. The more we know, the better. Yet at the end of the day, it's not our knowledge and precise doctrine that fulfill the Great Commission, proves that we genuinely know God, or affirms our love of him. It's obedience.

Unfortunately, when doctrine begins to replace obedience as the bull's-eye of discipleship, it's not long until a simple understanding of the gospel is considered inadequate for spiritual maturity. And when that happens, we've veered far off course.

Disdaining Childlike Faith

The moment a robust theology becomes the primary measure of spiritual maturity, we end up with a definition of discipleship that is within the reach of only the highly educated. Reading, reflecting, and the ability to nuance complex ideas becomes the prerequisite for spiritual maturity. Little children, the illiterate, and the uneducated need not apply.[20]

Devaluing Love

In addition, when doctrine trumps obedience it's not long until love gets shoved aside. If you haven't noticed, despite Jesus's clear command that we love one another, love is often the first casualty in our theological debates.

Consider the difference between the way we handle

our debates and the way the Apostle Paul handled the theological tension between those who felt it was okay to eat meat that had once been offered to idols and those who felt it was improper for a Christ follower.

When asked to settle the argument as to who was right and who was wrong, he gave the one answer neither side expected.

He said it didn't matter.

In essence, he dodged the question by reminding them that obeying Jesus's command to love one another was far more important than being right about eating meat previously sacrificed to an idol. He refused to give them a definitive answer. He simply told them:

> Now about food sacrificed to idols: We know that, "We all possess knowledge." But knowledge puffs up while love builds up . . . Whatever you believe about these things, keep between yourself and God.[21]

His answer must have driven them nuts. But Paul knew that despite their quest for an answer and a rule for every occasion, what they needed most was to simply obey Jesus's command to love one another.

We find the same priority of love in Jesus's letter to the church in Ephesus and Paul's definition of love in 1 Corinthians 13. The best doctrine without love is worthless.[22]

Stopping Hearsay

None of this is to say that heretical doctrine should be overlooked. The Apostle Paul's letters to the church at Colossi and the church at Galatia were both written to correct dangerous and goofy doctrine.

His warnings were stern. At one point he even told the Galatians that if they didn't abandon their Judaizing doctrines, Christ would be of no benefit to them.[23]

That's a strong statement. Obviously, he considered doctrine to be important. But at the end of the day, obedience is still the bull's-eye. I guarantee you that if my three mentors with stellar doctrine but poor obedience had instead had an immature understanding of doctrine and stellar obedience, Jesus would have been pleased.

So would their wives and children.

Gift Projection

One of the major forces behind the subtle shift from obedience to doctrine is something I call *Gift Projection.* It occurs when we begin to think that everyone is just like us—or will be when they finally grow up. We assume that if others knew what we know and experienced what we've experienced, they'd see the world just like we see it.[24]

Since pastors and Bible teachers are generally the ones who have a platform to describe what a disciple and spiritual maturity look like, it should come as no surprise that they most often describe it in terms of their own spiritual journey.

Unfortunately, the unintended consequence of allowing seminary-educated pastors and teachers define what it means to be a mature disciple is that our definitions now tend to bear a strong resemblance to seminary-educated pastors and teachers.

That works well for a church full of college graduates, but not so well for everyone else.

Back to Obedience

When I began to realize that a solid grasp of core (and not so core) doctrines had begun to replace simple obedience as my primary discipleship goal, I made a subtle change in the way I taught the Bible. It enabled me to realign my discipleship bull's-eye with the target that Jesus gave us in the Great Commission. It put obedience back in its rightful place.

I offer it by way of description, not prescription. But it has made a huge difference for both me and the church I serve.

I no longer see my primary job in preaching as merely teaching the biblical text. I see it as instructing people how to live the Christian life with the Bible as my only authority. It's a subtle shift. But it keeps my eyes on obedience.

I'm no longer satisfied with presenting facts about the text, its history, and its meaning. I'm not satisfied until I've figured out the "so what?" and how we can live in light of it. And every passage has one.

For instance, consider one of the great theological passages of the New Testament, Philippians 2:6-11. Known as the *kenosis* passage, it describes Jesus's *kenosis* (emptying of himself) as he left the glories of heaven to become a man headed for the cross.

If we approach this passage with a primarily doctrinal focus, the emphasis will be on the Greek word *kenoo* and the paradoxes that arise because the Bible presents Jesus as both fully God and fully man.

How can that be?

Volumes have been written trying to answer that question. Heated debates and church councils have struggled to come up with an answer. Was he God in a bod? Did he actually empty himself of his deity or was it simply veiled? Could he have accessed it at any time? Was his temptation genuine? Could he have sinned? And the list goes on.

Yet a careful look at the context of this passage reveals that Paul wasn't trying to give us a doctrinal treatise about Jesus's divinity and humanity. He was giving us an illustration of what it means to put the needs and interests of others above our own. Here's the *kenosis* passage in full context:

> Do nothing out of selfish ambition or vain conceit. Rather, in humility value others above yourselves, not looking to your own interests but each of you to the interests of the others. *In your relationships with one another, have the same mindset as Christ Jesus*:

> Who, being in very nature God, did not consider equality with God something to be used to his own advantage; rather, *he made himself nothing (Greek: kenoo)* by taking the very nature of a servant, being made in human likeness. And being found in appearance as a man, he humbled himself by becoming obedient to death—even death on a cross! Therefore God exalted him to the highest place and gave him the name that is above every name, that at the name of Jesus every knee should bow, in heaven and on earth and under the earth, and every tongue acknowledge that Jesus Christ is Lord, to the glory of God the Father.[25]

In other words, Paul was commanding them (and us) to obey Jesus's command that we love one another and our neighbor as we love ourselves.

His primary goal was not doctrine. It was obedience.

Perhaps that's why he wrote to remind a young pastor named Timothy that, "All Scripture is God-breathed and is useful for teaching, rebuking, correcting and training in righteousness, so that the servant of God may be thoroughly equipped for every good work."[26]

He wanted to make sure that Timothy understood the bull's-eye, that at the end of the day discipleship is all about obedience.

Chapter Six
SUBTLE SHIFT #3
From Persuasion to Warfare

Ask any non-Christian what comes to their mind when they hear the word "Christian," and my bet is that you won't hear anything about love or winsomeness.

If they know you're a Christian, odds are the answer will be innocuous, politically correct, and socially acceptable. It's not polite to blast someone to their face. But if you present yourself as a non-Christian asking another non-Christian, you might be shocked at what you hear.

Arrogant

Judgmental

Brainwashed

Intolerant

Angry

Bigots

Loners

Weird

Republican

These are just a few of the descriptors that I've heard over the years. Literally, no one has used the words loving, winsome, honest, dependable, or caring. And many non-Christians I talk to seem to think that the primary agenda of Christians is to impose our values and standards upon them.

Frankly, I know many Christians who think the same thing. Somehow their focus has subtly shifted over the years from persuading the lost to follow Jesus to winning the culture wars.

The unintentional result has been a stiffened resistance to the gospel. Non-Christians don't want to live like Christians. When they think we're trying to force them to live by our standards and values, they hunker down and fight back.

And when they're hunkered down or fighting back, there's one thing they never do.

Listen.

No one stops to listen to their enemies in the middle of battle.

The New Testament Model

Jesus commanded his followers to go out and recruit other followers. He never told them to create a Christian nation, impose outward forms of righteousness upon non-believers, or to preserve a particular culture. He told them to win over the lost. Their bull's-eye was persuasion. It was never cultural warfare.

We must not forget that the New Testament church was birthed in a cultural and political cesspool. There were no family values. Sexual perversion was normative, human life cheap, and justice nonexistent for anyone except the rich and powerful.

And even though Rome tolerated most foreign religions, it didn't tolerate Christianity. The early church suffered fierce cultural opposition and horrible persecution. All but one of the apostles died a martyr's death.

Yet none of the New Testament letters say anything about what we would call cultural warfare. And the passages that deal with spiritual warfare are always framed in the context of personal spirituality and righteousness. The focus of the early church was on changing hearts, not changing culture.

Now admittedly, when you change enough hearts, you change culture. But the reverse doesn't hold true. Changing culture doesn't change hearts. It results in grudging conformity. It causes people to play along on the outside while rebelling on the inside. It inoculates against the real disease, creating an abundance of the kind of lukewarm spirituality found in the church at Laodicea.[27]

Now I'm not suggesting that we stop seeking to bring God's redemptive power to our world or our culture. We need to be salt out of the saltshaker. I'm not saying that we should abandon politics. As long as we have the privilege of entering the public debate and influencing public policy, we should do so. If we flee the arena, we have no right to complain about what happens there.

But we must remember that cultural, legal, and political victories are not the bull's-eye that we're supposed to be aiming at. They are good things. But they are not the main thing. The main thing is winning the lost to Jesus. It's persuasion.

How Shift Happens

If you haven't noticed, there's always a crisis *du jour* in the Christian community.

Over time, some prove to be genuine.

Some prove to be nothing more than a boy crying, "Wolf!"

Does anyone remember Y2K?

Yet no matter what the crisis is (and whether it's genuine or bogus), there is always a great deal of pressure to make solving it or avoiding it our primary focus. Like many pastors, I'm constantly bombarded with emails, text messages, conversations, phone calls, and CDs that implore me to marshal my congregation to help with the latest cause.

But the moment we do so, we take our eye off the bull's-eye that Jesus gave us. You can't aim at two things at once. When our primary goal becomes to stop a misguided piece of legislation, pass a particular proposition, or win an election, evangelism and discipleship take a back seat. The bull's-eye shifts.

C. S. Lewis noted this dangerous slippery slope in his book, *The Screwtape Letters*.[28] It tells the story of a senior demon instructing a junior demon in how to mess up a Christian. The senior demon recommends that junior push his subject toward a hot-button political issue. It doesn't matter which one or which side of the issue he lands on. The important thing is to stir up his passion for the cause, because as long as he takes the bait an inevitable process will begin. What starts out as an important part of his religion will soon become the most important part of his religion, and not long after that, more important than his religion.

Lewis was right. I've watched it happen time after time to friends, members of my own church, and the church at large. Once we take our eyes off the bull's-eye that Jesus gave us, we start aiming our arrows at a bull's-eye not of his choosing. And it's not long until we don't even notice that we're completely missing the mark he asked us to hit.

How focused have we become on politics and winning the culture wars? So much so that many Christians are now more likely to marry outside their faith than outside their political party.[29]

Yet Jesus chose a different tact. It's no mere accident of history that his handpicked apostles included two people from completely opposite political and cultural extremes: Simon the Zealot and Matthew the tax collector.

There couldn't have been two more unlikely roommates. Simon was part of a loosely knit collection of Jewish insurrectionists who chipped away at their Roman oppressors with guerrilla warfare. Matthew was a Jew who collected taxes from his fellow Jews to hand over to the Roman oppressors.

Yet somehow, Jesus proved to be bigger than either of their incredibly divergent political viewpoints. There was room in his kingdom for each of them. And he sought out each of them, not to change their political paradigm, but to change their heart.

Towards Realignment

To realign our passion and bull's-eye with Jesus's command to reach the lost, we must realign the way we think about those who advance the cause of the enemy. Non-Christians (even those who lead the enemy's parade) are not the enemy. They are *victims* of the enemy.

Victims need to be rescued.

Enemies need to be wiped out.

Which is why it's so important that we understand who the enemy is and who the victims are, and how God wants us to respond to each one. Two New Testament passages give clear guidance. They show us how God wants us to respond to those who live like hell and advance the cause of the enemy. The first one is found in 2 Timothy 2:24-26. It reads like this:

> And the Lord's servant must not be quarrelsome but must be kind to everyone, able to teach, not resentful. Opponents must be gently instructed, *in the*

*hope that God will grant them repentance leading them
to a knowledge of the truth, and that they will come to
their senses and escape from the trap of the devil, who
has taken them captive to do his will.*[30]

The first thing to note is that even with those who do
the will of Satan, our goal is to win them over. We
respond to them in the hope that God will grant them
repentance and a knowledge of the truth. Our goal is
persuasion.

The second thing to notice is attitude and specific
actions we're called to take. We are not to argue or
quarrel. We must be kind to *everyone.* We need to be
able to teach or explain the truth, but we can't be a bit
resentful or bitter at what they're doing or what has
happened.

Frankly, it's here that many of us miss the boat. As
we have continued to lose ground in the so-called
cultural wars, I've noticed increasing levels of
resentment, slander, rumormongering, and harsh
critiques that no one would characterize as being kind or
gentle.

It's no wonder we continue to lose ground. We're
aiming at the wrong target. We've failed to follow
God's game plan. We've sloughed aside persuasion in
favor of warfare. And we've tried to fight our spiritual
battles with the weapons of the flesh.

A second key passage is found in 1 Corinthians 5:9-
12. In it, the Apostle Paul tells us how to respond to the
non-Christians around us, especially those who are
living like hell. Here's what he says:

I wrote to you in my letter not to associate with
sexually immoral people—not at all meaning the
people of this world who are immoral, or the greedy
and swindlers, or idolaters. In that case you would have
to leave this world. But now I am writing to you that
you must not associate with anyone who claims to be a

brother or sister but is sexually immoral or greedy, an idolater or slanderer, a drunkard or swindler. Do not even eat with such people. What business is it of mine to judge those outside the church? Are you not to judge those inside?

Once again, note that the metaphor of spiritual warfare gets it all wrong.

You don't fraternize with the enemy.

But this passage tells us that we're supposed to hang around those who are immoral, greedy, swindlers, drunkards, or idolaters and don't know Jesus. It makes no sense when seen through the lens of cultural warfare. It makes perfect sense when seen through the lens of persuasion.

Without contact, we'd have no impact. Persuasion demands that we rub shoulders—and frankly, that we like one another. No one is ever persuaded by someone who looks down on them. If I sense that you don't like me (or worse, disdain me and what I stand for), there is no way that I'll listen when you tell me what soap to buy, much less how to vote, or what God to follow. I'll simply raise my defenses and shut you off.

According to this passage, the only people we are to cut off and stop associating with are fellow Christians who live like non-Christians. Everyone else is to be pursued with the goal of winning them over.

And if you think about it, isn't that what Jesus did for us? While we were still his enemies, he pursued us and died for us. He turned his enemies (and some of his chief persecutors) into sons and daughters. Now he asks us to continue to do the same.[31]

A Surprising Addition to the Family

A number of years ago, a middle-aged man came barging into my office. He demanded that I baptize him. And he wanted me to do it right then.

I had no idea who he was. So I asked him to calm down and tell me his story. I told him I wasn't in the habit of baptizing complete strangers within minutes of meeting them.

"You don't understand," he said. "I need to be baptized right now!"

"Right now?"

"Yes, right now," he explained.

"Can you tell me why?" I asked.

"I'm moving. Tomorrow," he said.

"Where?"

"Salt Lake City.

"I'll turn the water on," I said, "But first, you have to tell me your story."

He then explained that his marriage had been in deep weeds, and his wife had given him an ultimatum. They needed to start counseling, go to church, or do something to work on it, or she would leave. So he decided to try our church. He added that he worked for a newspaper.

"I'm part of the liberal media. I knew I was the enemy. So I sat in the back and waited for you to bash my friends and me, especially since we were in the middle of an election cycle.

"But you never did. All you talked about was Jesus and the Bible.

"A couple of months ago I said that prayer to start following Jesus. Then I got this great offer to be a managing editor in Salt Lake. I need to get baptized before we go."

So I baptized him.

A few years later he showed up again, this time at the front of the stage after a weekend service. He reintroduced himself and told me the rest of his story. He moved. He found a good church. He was now leading a small group Bible study, and his wife was in charge of the Sunday school ministry.

After he left, I pondered how different his story would have been if we'd fallen into the trap of trading persuasion for warfare. He would have come and sat in the back row of the church only to have his suspicions confirmed. He and his ilk were the enemy.

No doubt he would have shut down, stopped listening, and stopped coming.

We would have unwittingly aided and abetted the enemy by pushing someone who was on the verge of breaking free further into the darkness. Which sadly happens all too often when our target shifts from persuasion to warfare.

Chapter Seven
SUBTLE SHIFT #4
From People to Numbers

If you ask a fish, "How's the water?" he'll ask you, "What water?" It's all he knows. Everything he's ever seen or experienced has been within the water paradigm.

We're no different. We only know the world as we've experienced it. So we naturally tend to evaluate and understand everything through the lens of our personal experiences, including the way we interpret and understand the Bible.

I remember the first time I stood in the ruins of an ancient Jewish synagogue. I was shocked at how small it was. As a modern-day suburbanite, I had always imagined that the synagogues of Jesus's day were about the size of a mid-sized church. I hadn't factored in the fact that Jesus ministered in an era without easy mobility or that everyone who attended had to live within walking distance.

I also used to wonder why the New Testament never said anything about small groups or the importance of building and maintaining community. I failed to consider that the early church met in homes and that most people lived in well-defined neighborhoods they seldom left. A house church is a small group. It doesn't need to focus on building community. And the anonymity and superficiality that ail our modern-day churches are hardly problems in a small and stable neighborhood where everyone knows everyone—and has since birth.

But that's no longer the world we live in. The neighborhoods of the past no longer exist. They've been killed off by our mobility and replaced by new connection points: the workplace, special interest groups, and our station-in-life.

The change in our relational patterns has been so profound that we now value anonymity more than interconnectedness. So much so that the right to privacy has been deemed a constitutional right.

So what happened? How did it get this way?

For that, we can thank Henry Ford and his Model-T.

How the Automobile Changed Everything

The advent of automobile was a watershed event. It gave mobility to the middle class. But it was still a big-ticket item. Most middle-class families had just one car as recently as 50 years ago. But today, automobiles are ubiquitous. Since 2003 the U.S. has actually had more registered vehicles than licensed drivers.[32]

Make no mistake. This proliferation of the automobile has changed everything.

It has freed us from the constraints of our geographical neighborhood. We are no longer chained to the closest market, restaurant, hardware store, or church. If something that we deem better exists within a reasonable drive time, we drive to it. As a result, our cities, stores, and churches have grown far larger than ever before.

Big is the new normal.

Now I'm not bemoaning the loss of small. There are some good things that come with economy of scale. I'm glad that I can now choose the best instead of the closest. Whether I'm shopping or worshipping, I like having choices. But big does have some downsides.

The Downsides of Big

The first downside of larger cities, stores, and churches is found in increasingly shallow relationships. When everything grows huge, everyone becomes a stranger. Even in our churches, the quality and depth of relationships that the New Testament considers to be normal have become increasingly rare.

The second downside is lost perspective. We think of historically large churches as being small. In the past, any church over 200 was considered large. A congregation of 400 would put you on the map. It took just 800 members in 1920 to be included in Elmer Towns's classic church growth book, *The 10 Largest Sunday School Churches in the World*. And even as recently as 1970, there were only 10 churches reporting attendance of 2,000 or more.[33]

Now here's the problem with thinking you're small when you're not. It's easy for numerical growth to become priority No. 1. That's because when a church thinks of itself as small, it tends to assume that the community and relationships are already among its greatest strengths. And when that happens, adding more people quickly becomes more important than finishing the discipleship task.

But the truth is that any church over 150 is not the close-knit family it thinks it is. More often than not, it's a core of worker bees at the center that know and love each other deeply while everyone else circles around trying to connect.

That's why when the church I pastor reached 180 in attendance (kids and adults), we cut back on our large group meetings to focus on relationships and small groups. We realized that most of our relationships were casual and superficial. Not because there was something wrong with our people, but because we had too many people.

The New Testament lists more than 30 "one anothers" that describe the type of relationships and behaviors that are supposed to be normative in a local church. They include things like loving one another, bearing with one another, confessing our sins to one another, praying for one another, speaking to one another in psalms, hymns, and songs, and a host of other things that couldn't take place as long as our meetings and groupings were too large.

When People Become Numbers

Now I'm not saying that large churches are bad. I pastor a massive church with well over 10,000 people showing up each weekend. I'm simply saying that the moment our *primary* focus shifts from developing biblical community and iron-sharpening-iron relationships to growing the church larger, genuine discipleship becomes nearly impossible.

And the first sign that biblical community, life-on-on life relationships, and the discipleship that flows out of it are no longer a priority is when we stop keeping track of individuals. People become numbers.

There's no need to keep track of individuals in a house church. It happens naturally. It's the same for a church plant or church of 50 to 75. But somewhere around 125 to 150, we start to ask, "Have you seen Jason and Amy?" And no one can remember.

Churches at this size often try to institute some sort of system to track individuals. But I've found that somewhere around 300 to 400 most churches throw up their hands and decide that tracking individuals is too complex and difficult to do.

So they quit trying. *Total attendance* replaces *individual attendance* as the key metric. And when that happens, there's no longer any way to know if they're fulfilling the Great Commission or simply cycling an ever-changing crowd through a revolving door.

If we don't know who's coming, it's impossible to know who's growing.

Numbers Lie

Consider how misleading total attendance figures can be.

If all I track is total attendance instead of individual attendance and my church grows from 400 to 500, I'll see it as a great year. But if what really happened was a loss of 100 people and a gain of 200 new ones? That's a lousy year.

One calls for, "Hallelujah! We grew by 25 percent!"

The other calls for, "Oh No! We lost 25 percent!"

This subtle shift from tracking individuals to counting numbers leads many churches to think they are healthy and growing when in reality they are simply a revolving door with a bigger front door than back door.

Coaching Blind

Imagine a baseball coach who only kept track of the final score and never paid attention to the box score. He'd have a hard time winning many games without knowing who struck out and who hit home runs.

Yet that's exactly what happens in many of our churches. We have no box score. We have no accurate method of tracking individuals. And even when they try, our information is often incomplete, inaccurate, or hopelessly out of date.

But it doesn't have to be that way.

Counting the Offering

Every church I know of counts the money that comes in. They count it weekly. They count it to the penny. At the end of the year, they send out a receipt for IRS purposes. It lists a donor's contributions in detail.

No one gets a letter saying, "Thank you for your generous donation of somewhere between $300 and $30,000."

Now that's not easy to do. It takes accountants, staff members, and lots of donuts for all the volunteers who help count and record the offering. But somehow every church finds a way to get it done and get it right. Which tells me that in many of our churches money must be more important than people. Because we'll do whatever it takes to track where our money comes from to the penny, but we can't tell you who was in a small group or Sunday school class last week.

Staying Focused on People

I've never been willing to accept the inevitability of shifting from tracking people to tracking numbers. That's why back when North Coast Church was less than 200 in attendance, we made a decision to do whatever it took to carefully track our small group and weekend attendance.

Frankly, it wasn't long until it became clear that it was impossible for us to accurately track individual worship service attendance. Even with a strong push each weekend, the best we can get is a 50 to 60 percent response. Nonetheless, 50 to 60 percent is better than 0 percent. So we take what we can get and carefully record and track all the cards that are turned in. It's a laborious task. But it's well worth it if we really believe that people who come are more important than the money they give.

As for our small groups, it's much easier. Since we treat them as the hub of our ministry, we have high participation. This year it's equal to 94 percent of our average weekend attendance. And I can tell you in real time who was in a group last week.

How do we do it?

It starts with the conviction that tracking individuals is more important than money. If we didn't really believe that, we wouldn't go to all the trouble to chase down those who forget to turn in their attendance.

And believe me, at times it's a hassle.

But when Mrs. Jones writes a check and we can't read the number or the amount, we don't throw away her check. We contact her to find out how much it's supposed to be. In the same way, we actively pursue (some would say hound) those who fail to turn in their attendance.

So here's what it might look like in a real-world scenario.

Pursuing What's Important

Imagine that you're leading a Tuesday evening small group. On Tuesday night you should receive an automated text or email reminder to turn in your attendance.

On Wednesday morning a small group volunteer or staff member gets an email dashboard showing which Tuesday night groups turned in their attendance and which ones didn't. If you didn't turn in your attendance and a brief description of what happened in the group, you'll get a text message or phone call. If you don't respond by the end of the day, you'll get a call on your cell phone—at work.

Most likely you'll say, "I'm sorry, I'll do it when I get home."

"Okay" is the wrong response.

The right response is to say, "Don't worry, it will take just a couple of seconds." Then the volunteer or staff member should quickly go down the list asking who was there and who missed. As to the description of what happened this week, they'll skip it.

The whole process should take less than 90 seconds. And I guarantee you that after you've been called once or twice, you won't need to be called again. You'll realize that we really do keep real-time attendance.

And even if you're the type who always forgets, you'll be called each week. Not in annoyance, but with gratitude that you lead a group. After all, we wouldn't be annoyed at Mrs. Jones if we had to ask her how much her check was for every week. We'd gladly chase her down and make the deposit.

Keeping People in the Bull's-Eye

Admittedly, it's no easy thing to accurately track individual attendance and involvement. In light of the difficulty and complexity, it's understandable why so many churches make the shift to counting numbers instead of people.

But we can't settle for numbers if we want to fulfill the Great Commission. Numbers can't be discipled. Only people can be discipled.

Fortunately, along with the huge increase in churches with more than 200 attendees, there has also been an explosion of church management software and programs that can make what once would have been a gargantuan task, manageable. If you don't have one (or don't like the one you have), you might want to check out Church Community Builder. They are one of the best and one of the gracious sponsors of this book. They can be reached at ChurchCommunityBuilder.com.

For real-time small group attendance, you might want to check out the attendance tracking and small group dashboard that MortarStone Analytics offers. It can function as a stand-alone program for smaller churches or integrate seamlessly with most existing church management programs.

At the end of the day, it doesn't matter how we do it. We can use old-school pen and paper. We can use the latest and greatest software solution. We can intentionally plant smaller churches that multiply. Or we can grow massive megachurches with complex tracking systems. But one way or the other we have to ensure that our people don't become mere numbers. Because when they do, it won't be long until discipleship is something we talk about but have no earthly idea if it's actually happening.

Chapter Eight
SUBTLE SHIFT #5
From Jesus to Justice

The pursuit of justice is important. It's not an extra-credit option for the super committed. It's core to what it means to follow Jesus. We have no right to call ourselves disciples if we turn a deaf ear to the suffering and injustices that surround us.

The Bible says that mercy is more important than sacrifice. We're required to act justly and love mercy; and those of us who ignore the cries of the poor will one day cry out ourselves and not be answered.[34]

Yet as important as mercy and justice may be, they aren't the main thing.

Jesus is the main thing.

Unfortunately, in some of our circles there's been a subtle shift away from the main thing. Justice has replaced Jesus as the new North Star. First priority is no longer bringing Jesus to a lost and dying world. It's bringing mercy and justice to a suffering and disadvantaged world. Jesus has become an optional add-on.

I know of one self-described Christian organization that has gone so far as to intentionally bury the name of

Jesus any time the people they are trying to help find Jesus offensive. It's an organization that does lots of good deeds. But it's a stretch to say that they do them in the name of Jesus if he's only mentioned when it's convenient or helpful for fundraising.

It's also a long way from the model Jesus followed when he sent out his followers to heal the sick and proclaim the coming kingdom. He told them to stay when welcomed but to shake the dust off their feet anywhere they weren't welcomed as his emissaries.[35]

The shift from offering mercy and justice in the name of Jesus to offering mercy and justice without mentioning his name may seem subtle. After all, we're still doing the things he has called us to do. But it's a subtle shift with huge consequences.

The moment Jesus becomes optional, the Great commission has been redefined. Jesus didn't command us to go into all the world offering mercy and fighting for justice. He commanded us to go into all the world making disciples.

Granted, disciples who obey everything Jesus commanded will champion mercy and justice. But it's a mercy and justice that flows out of following Jesus. It's a mercy and justice that's offered in his name.

Who Is That Masked Man?

This subtle shift reminds me of a popular TV show from the 1950s. It featured a masked hero named the Lone Ranger. He would ride into town to save the day and then ride off into the sunset. As he rode off, the people he had just rescued would suddenly realize that they hadn't gotten his name.

They'd ask, "Who was that masked man?"

But it was always too late. He was long gone. They never got his name.

In the same way, justice without Jesus leaves people

better off. It may even save lives. But if we leave and they have no idea who Jesus is (and have had no opportunity to hear more should they choose), we've done nothing to help them with life's biggest problem: the sin that we all will have to give account for someday.

In the words of Jesus, "What good is it for someone to gain the whole world but forfeit his soul?"[36]

The Jesus Model

It's impossible to imagine a Jesus who didn't go around healing and helping those in need.

He always brought mercy and justice.

But he also brought the gospel. Every time.

His miracles served a larger purpose. They drew the crowd, authenticated his claims, and teed up his message, so much so that he told the people who didn't believe his words to believe in him because of his miracles.[37]

There is no evidence that Jesus ever came to town and healed the sick, fed the hungry, and then moved on without letting people know who he was and why he'd come. Justice and mercy were important parts of his agenda. But they weren't his agenda. Salvation was.

Fact is, Jesus sometimes walked away from desperate needs. The one who taught us the parable of the Good Samaritan even walked by some hurting people without lifting a hand. I know it's hard to believe. But that's what the Bible says.

Leaving the Needy to Proclaim the Message

Once when he was in the town of Capernaum, word spread about his healings. That evening a large crowd gathered. When they came, he healed them. The next morning an even larger crowd showed up. They included many lame, sick, and diseased. Their needs were legit and desperate. But Jesus was nowhere to be found.

He'd risen very early in the morning and headed off to a solitary place to pray. When Simon and his disciples finally found him, they urged him to return to the waiting crowd. They needed him. They'd been waiting all morning.

But Jesus brushed them off and said, "Let us go somewhere else, to the nearby villages, so that I can preach there also. That is why I have come." So they headed off to the villages of Galilee.[38]

Walking by a Crippled Beggar

Or consider the crippled man that Peter healed on the temple steps. One day as Peter was walking to the temple a disabled beggar asked him for money. Peter said that he had none, but what he had he would give to the man. So he told him to rise up and walk in the name of Jesus Christ of Nazareth.

Then he reached out, took him by the right hand, and helped him up. Instantly the man's legs were healed.

It's a beautiful story of mercy. The man had been lame since birth. Every day for 40 years he had been carried to the temple steps to beg alms from those entering the temple. Now thanks to Peter's ministry he was walking, jumping, and praising God in the very temple courts that he'd been unable to enter for his entire lifetime.

But don't miss something important in this story. If he'd been lame since birth and had been carried every day for 40 years to the temple steps, Jesus must have walked right by him numerous times without lending a hand.[39]

How can that be?

He obviously had the power to heal.

Why wouldn't he use it?

The answer is that Jesus had a mission greater than

bringing mercy and justice to every evil and wrong he encountered. His mission wasn't to bring temporary mercy and justice to the disadvantaged, the beaten down, and the infirm. It was to bring eternal mercy and justice to those who would follow him.

To follow him, they had to know who he was. They had to know what he offered. They had to hear the gospel so they could decide one way or the other.

Jesus's earthy miracles and healings weren't the core of his ministry. They were mere samplers, appetizers, a foretaste of the far greater mercy and justice that awaits all who follow him.

That explains why when his disciples came back from a road trip pumped that they'd been able to cast out demons and heal the sick, he told them that they were rejoicing over the wrong things. Far more important was the fact that their names were written in heaven.[40]

Aligning Justice With Jesus

I think I've made it clear that whenever we become more passionate about justice than Jesus, we've veered off course. But having said that, I also want to be clear that we can't claim to be genuinely passionate about Jesus without offering justice. The two go together. They can't be separated.

At North Coast Church we were missional before it was called missional. We have a long history of serving our community and meeting the needs of the disadvantaged. We average a couple of community service projects a day. We periodically close down all of our weekend services to spend the weekend blessing our local schools, community service organizations, and others who help the needy. In a 48-hour time span, we'll complete more than 200-plus projects and provide more than $2 million in goods and services.

Along the way, we've been recognized with countless awards. We've seen the attitude of the community, politicians, and non-Christians toward our church and Christians change. But at the end of the day, the most important thing we've done is open doors to share the gospel.[41]

We *share* the love of Jesus with no strings attached. But we do it in the hope that we will one day have the opportunity to *explain* the love of Jesus.

After all, if Jesus is the way, truth and life, and no one can come to the Father except through him, it's the only thing that makes sense.[42] To share the love of Jesus without seeking a chance to explain the love of Jesus is like coming up with a miracle cancer cure and not telling anyone about it.

The Lens of History

There's an old saying that those who don't know history are bound to repeat it. When it comes to justice without Jesus, no one seems to be reading the history books.

Within the last century the Roman Catholic Church was sidetracked in Latin America by the shift from Jesus to justice. What began as an attempt to minister to the poor by freeing them from unjust economic, social, and political structures morphed into something that had nothing to do with Jesus, the cross, or the resurrection. In its heyday (the 1950s to 1970s) this new focus, called Liberation Theology, pushed the message of the cross aside and aligned itself with anyone and anything that helped advance the cause of the poor and socially marginalized, including Marxism and guerrilla warfare.

Then, just as Liberation Theology began to wane in the Catholic Church, our American mainline denominations decided to pick up the torch. Many of these mainline churches began to set aside Jesus and the gospel to focus on helping the poor and changing political and structural injustices. Leading with Jesus was seen as being exclusive and spiritually self-centered. Social justice (an important biblical imperative) became the new ministry North Star. Jesus and evangelism became optional.

It wasn't long until many of their churches began to hemorrhage members. It should have been no surprise. Without Jesus, they'd turned into nothing more than a religiously nostalgic community service organization.

Bizarrely, many evangelicals have now decided to walk down the same path, thinking that this time it will somehow take them to a different destination.

It won't.

Towards Realignment

Now the centrality of Jesus, the cross, and the resurrection doesn't mean that every good deed has to be followed by a spiritual timeshare presentation. People don't have to agree up front to listen to be worthy of our help. We're to follow the example of Jesus who died for us while we were still in our sins and positioned as his enemies. We are called to take the first step toward those in need.[43]

But to think that we can carry out our calling and advance his kingdom while pushing aside Jesus and the gospel message is to seriously misunderstand the purpose of his coming.

Justice without Jesus isn't kingdom work. It's social work.

The bull's-eye of our calling is not providing mercy and justice where it's needed; it's to recruit followers of Jesus, teaching them to obey all that he taught, and then deploying them into kingdom service. Life is too short and hell too hot to let anything crowd out Jesus and the cross.

Chapter Nine
REALIGNMENT
Fixing What's Gone Wrong

It's no news flash that the impact of biblical Christianity in America has been steadily declining for decades. You'd have to stick your head in the sand not to notice. Polls, surveys, and statistics consistently show a waning influence.

The press, the educated elite, and the culture have increasingly marginalized us. Many see the church as a collection of narrow-minded, intolerant historical preservationists dedicated to holding back social progress. In some cases, we've begun to face low-level persecution. And many believe full-scale persecution is just around the corner.

From Respect to Dismissive Silence

I fly a lot. And I've found that you can learn a lot at 30,000 feet.

When my kids were young and the ministry of North Coast was less known, I didn't travel much. But as our church began to grow and I began writing books, outside ministry opportunities started to open up. Next thing I knew, I was on the speaking circuit.

Then one day my oldest son (who was seven at the time) told my wife, "I don't like it when dad writes because he doesn't play with me."

Bingo. That night we decided that I wouldn't write any more books until all of our kids were in college. So I took a 15-year hiatus from writing and most outside speaking gigs to focus on being a dad and a pastor. I wanted to make sure my own kids loved Jesus, loved the local church, and thought it was great having a dad who was a pastor. I saw no value in impacting the church at large while risking the loss of the most important congregation God had assigned me to shepherd.

Thankfully, God answered our prayers. My grown sons and daughter love Jesus, the local church, and think having a dad who is a pastor had some cool perks.

But when it came time for me to re-engage with my writing and larger kingdom ministry, I was shocked at how radically attitudes had changed toward churches and pastors. During that time, I'd lived in my own little bubble. I only knew the response that our local community had toward our church and my role as a pastor. I'd lost touch with the changing attitudes within our culture at large toward the generic church and the stereotypical pastor.

Who knows? Maybe if I'd been traveling all that time I still wouldn't have noticed. It's hard to recognize a slow and steady change. But with 15 years between measurements, the changes were obvious.

Like many pastors, I have always dodged telling new acquaintances what I do for a living. The moment they find out, the conversation changes. Their language cleans up, and they look at me as if I'm going to make an altar call or take an offering.

Yet no matter what I do to avoid the subject, once the conversation engages, sooner or later they are going to ask me what I do for a living. At that point I have to tell them I'm a pastor or lie. So I tell them I'm a writer. Then after I'm overwhelmed with guilt, I come clean. I tell them I'm a pastor.

Years ago the typical response was respectful and mildly affirming. Even if their language up to that point indicated that they'd never set foot in a church; they'd find some way to connect spiritually. They'd let me know that they had a brother, uncle, or long-lost cousin who was a pastor or missionary. Sometimes they'd even start telling me about the church they went to. That is until I'd ask them the name of the pastor. Then they'd have a sudden case of dementia. Which is understandable. I can't remember people I met 10 years ago on Easter either.

But after my 15-year break from flying around the country, I noticed a significant change. This time when my seatmates found out that I was a pastor, there was much less effort to connect. They'd still clean up their language. But instead of trying to impress me that they were somehow connected to a church, they'd tell me a story about why they no longer went to church or never did in the first place. There was still a small measure of respect for my role and position as a pastor. But it was grudging at best.

Now today, the typical response is anything but respect. Once they find out that I'm a pastor, there's an awkward silence followed by a quick change in topic. If they find out I pastor a so-called megachurch, it's even worse. The conversation shuts down completely. I might as well have said that I'm a recently released sex-offender on my way back home from prison.

So what happened?

How did we lose so much ground so fast?

I believe there are lots of reasons. Many of them are beyond the scope of this book. But we can place a significant portion of the blame on the long-term cumulative effects of the five subtle shifts we've been looking at.

Little By Little Over a Long Time Makes a Big Difference

The problem with mission creep is that it's subtle and slow. No one notices. But given enough time, the smallest shift can take us far off course.

I believe that's what's happened with these five subtle shifts. No one meant to get off track. Everything was well-intended. But these shifts have slowly sabotaged and undercut our ability to fulfill the Great Commission. They've replaced biblical evangelism and discipleship with glitzy counterfeits that look good but lack the power to genuinely transform lives or our communities.

Each has played its own unique role in our crumbling influence and impact.

For instance, the shift from making disciples to getting as many decisions for Christ as possible has caused many people to think they're Christians when they're not. It has also filled our churches with people who believe that carefully following Jesus is an extra-credit option for those who are really into it. It's killed our credibility. Our behavior and moral standards have ceased to be any different from the culture at large. We become salt without saltiness. And with that, we've lost our ability to impact and influence the people we rub shoulders with.

The drift from obedience to doctrine has also done

great damage. It has created an elitist spirituality that is out of reach for all but the highly educated or intellectually inquisitive. It has produced an arrogance where longtime and studious Christians look down on those who don't yet know everything they know. Rather than drawing people in, it pushes them away. Worse, it has divided us up into warring tribes, battling over our differing understandings of difficult and debatable Bible passages. And as we've lost our unity, we've lost our power.

In a similar fashion, the shift from persuasion to warfare has crippled our ability to evangelize. Our increasingly harsh rhetoric has caused many non-Christians (especially those who live or support a non-Christian agenda) to assume that they are our enemy and that our goal is to wipe them out, not win them over. It's no wonder that they've gone on a counteroffensive once they perceived they had the upper hand. That's what you do when you're at war.

The transition from focusing on people to focusing on numbers has resulted in large churches without accountability or any means to measure spiritual progress. The crowd has replaced the church. As a result, the "one-anothers" of scripture have been relegated to something we teach about but seldom experience. It's no wonder that the world no longer says, "My, how they love one another." After all, we don't even *know* one another anymore.

And finally, the shift from bringing Jesus to the lost to bringing justice to the oppressed has buried the centrality of the gospel. If we never tell people who don't know about Jesus about him, they'll never follow Jesus. And if we really believe that justice without Jesus is enough to fulfill our calling, then the Great Commission has lost all meaning and Jesus has become just one of many options for knowing God.

Added together, these five subtle shifts have had a disastrous impact. They've slowly eroded our message, our influence, and our credibility.

So what can we do to right the ship?

Towards Realignment

To realign our priorities with Jesus and the Great Commission, we'll have to first step back and take stock. Then we'll have to replace our current targets with the original bull's-eyes that Jesus gave us: making disciples, obedience, persuasion, individuals, and Jesus.

But that's not easy. The inertia that comes with mission creep is strong.

Zero-Basing

At North Coast Church, one of the most powerful tools we've used to help us keep our eyes on the target and regularly make the adjustments needed has been a process called "zero-basing."

A zero-based meeting or retreat gathers a small group of key leaders and simply asks:

What would we do differently if we were starting all over?

If there were no backlash to worry about, what would we drop?

What would we start?

What would we change?

How does the reality of our ministry match with our stated vision and goals?

What would we do differently if our only boundary was a radical commitment to the Great Commission?

We've used zero-based meetings and retreats to evaluate how we're doing. We'll put our entire ministry or a specific program or ministry under the microscope. The clarity that comes from stepping back to ask these kinds of questions is amazing. We almost always head home with some significant changes in mind.

Where Are We?

The first step in a zero-based meeting is to honestly assess where we are. If no one realizes that we've drifted, everyone thinks we're on target.

If you don't know where to begin, you might consider using a book like Will Mancini's *Church Unique*. It can help any church or leadership team discover where they are, their unique positioning in the kingdom, and what it will take for them to fulfill their unique role in fulfilling the Great Commission.[44]

The same goes for this book. It's designed to help leaders and teams ask tough questions:

What are we aiming at?

What are we actually hitting?

What needs to change?

But frankly, anything you use to help you ask and answer these kinds of tough questions about the alignment of your mission and methods will be incredibly helpful and clarifying.

The sad truth is that most churches and ministries never stop to compare their results with their target. They keep right on drifting under the assumption that as long as people show up and the bills are paid, God is at work.

Where to Next?

After reading a book like this or zero-basing your ministry in light of the Great Commission, it can be tempting to try and change everything—all at once. But never forget that leadership is the art of the possible. It's not the art of the ideal.

And it's here that realignment can go bad.

A wise leader doesn't risk blowing up the church Jesus died for just because it's drifted off course. Even the church at Laodicea got one more warning. A wise and godly leader nudges a church or ministry back in the right direction as quickly as possible—with the key words being *"as quickly as possible."*

Sometimes simply stopping the drift is a big win. Sometimes inching everyone a little closer to target is all that can be accomplished at the moment. That's okay. Jesus took three years to get his inner circle aligned. And even then, they didn't get it all right.

It took the American church a long time to get so far off course. It's going to take a while for us to get back on course. My hope is that this book will make a small contribution to the process of realigning our methods and ministries with the target Jesus gave us, and that it will help churches and leadership teams honestly access (1) where they are, (2) what they're been aiming at, and (3) what they've been hitting.

Because only then can we accurately recalibrate and realign with the proper target: *Going into all the world, making disciples, baptizing them, and teaching them to obey everything Jesus taught us.*

Notes

Notes

Notes

Additional Books by Larry Osborne

LEADERSHIP

INNOVATIONS DIRTY LITTLE SECRET

Most books on innovation make it sound as if successful innovation is the end result of a carefully followed recipe. But the simple fact is that when it comes to any new venture, failure is the surest horse to bet on.

STICKY TEAMS

Serving as a church leader can be a tough assignment. Whatever your role, odds are you've known your share of the frustration, conflict, and disillusionment that comes with silly turf battles, conflicting vision, and marathon meetings. No doubt, you've asked yourself, 'How did it get this way?'

STICKY CHURCH

In Sticky Church, author and pastor Larry Osborne makes the case that closing the back door of your church is even more important than opening the front door wider. He offers a time-tested strategy for doing so: sermon-based small groups that dig deeper into the weekend message and tightly velcro members to the ministry.

THE UNITY FACTOR

It's no secret that church boards can be a source of conflict and that healthy staff teams are a rarity. In The Unity Factor (Larry Osborne's first book and the leadership classic), Larry walks us through the process and principles that turned North Coast's conflict ridden board and staff into a healthy and thriving leadership team.

DISCIPLESHIP/SPIRITUAL FORMATION

ACCIDENTAL PHARISEES

Zealous faith can have a dangerous, dark side. While recent calls for radical Christians have challenged many to be more passionate about their faith, the down side can be a budding arrogance and self-righteousness that "accidentally" sneaks into our outlook.

10 DUMB THINGS SMART CHRISTIANS BELIEVE

People don't set out to build their faith upon myths and spiritual urban legends. But somehow such falsehoods keep showing up in the way that many Christians think about life and God.

SPIRITUALITY FOR THE REST OF US

If you've ever wondered why all the books on spirituality and the inner life are written by introverts with big vocabularies; if you find that you or those around you don't fit the mold; if you've grown weary of one-size-fits-all formulas for spiritual growth – then this book is for you.

For information on bulk orders,
please contact Erica Brandt at
Erica@northcoastchurch.com

YOU'RE CALLED TO EQUIP.

HOW?

Equipping begins by engaging people, providing useful tools and empowering them to lead. If your church management software is not helping you equip and empower your leaders, perhaps it's time for a new tool.

Visit churchcommunitybuilder.com to learn more.

 CHURCH COMMUNITY BUILDER   SOFTWARE | COACHING | TRIBES

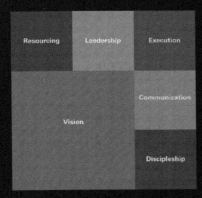

≡XPONENTIAL
RESOURCING CHURCH PLANTERS

- Largest annual church planting conference in the world (Orlando & Los Angeles)
- 50+ FREE eBooks
- 400+ Hours of FREE audio training via podcasts from national leaders
- FREE weekly email newsletter
- Future Travelers learning communities
- Church planters blog
- Conference content available via Digital Access Pass

exponential.org ›

@churchplanting
info@exponential.org

NORTH COAST TRAINING

helps you **CRAFT STRONG, STABLE MINISTRIES** that prepares your church to **BREAKTHROUGH** barriers, **OVERCOME** plateaus, and **PRIME FOR GROWTH.**

We teach, train, coach, and consult with church leaders in the following areas:

- Small Group Ministry
- Multi-Venue/Multi-Site Ministry
- Healthy Leadership Teams & Leadership Development
- *Plus, much more!*

Calvary Baptist was seeking to develop a small group culture when we attended training at North Coast. We followed up with coaching and consulting led by Chris Mavity who helped us process and develop a successful small group launch. We started 19 new gatherings and had over 30 % of our folks in Life Groups in just one year. We are developing a culture of FUN, FOCUS and FRIENDSHIPS through the guidance of the Holy Spirit and ongoing care and partnership with the North Coast Training Team.

Chet Anderson,
Executive Pastor,
Calvary Baptist

REGISTER TODAY for a FREE ministry consult!
(760) 724-6700

northcoasttraining.org

Notes

[1] Matthew 28:19-20
[2] 1 Peter 4:10-11/ Colossians 3:17
[3] Colossians 1:28-29
[4] Matthew 16:18
[5] 1 Corinthians 9:22-23
[6] Matthew 10:17-27
[7] 1 John 2:3-6
[8] 1 Peter 2:12
[9] 1 Peter 4:4
[10] *National & International Religion Report*, Vol. 4 #21, October 8, 1990, page 8
[11] Matthew 16:18
[12] John 19:38
[13] Matthew 28:19-20
[14] Matthew 21:28-31
[15] Osborne, Larry, *Ten Dumb Things Smart Christians Believe*. Multnomah Books, 2009
[16] Matthew 28:19-20 italics added for emphasis
[17] 1 John 2:3-5 italics added for emphasis
[18] John 14:15
[19] 2 Timothy 3:16-17
[20] 1 Corinthians 1:20-29 and Luke 18:16
[21] 1 Corinthians 8:1 and Romans 14:1-22
[22] Revelation 2:1-7, I Corinthians 13:1-13, & Matthew 22:36-40
[23] Galatians 5:1-6
[24] For more on Gift Projection see my books: *Accidental Pharisees*, 2012, Zondervan and *Spirituality For The Rest of Us*, 2007, Multnomah
[25] Philippians 2:3-11
[26] 2 Timothy 3:16-17
[27] Revelation 3:14-22
[28] Lewis, C. S., *The Screwtape Letters*, 2009, HarperOne, reprint.
[29] Williamson, Elizabeth, *THE WALL STREET JOURNAL*, Life & Culture: The Dating Game Gets Partisan, With Politics a Deal Breaker Opposites Aren't So Attractive; Voting Record Trumps Religion, Looks and Schooling, Updated October 28, 2012, http://online.wsj.com/news/articles/SB10001424052970203872204578069373224970996

[30] 2 Timothy 2:24-26 italics added for emphasis

[31] Romans 5:10

[32] *Road & Track*, 2003, More Cars Than Licensed Drivers, (http://www.roadandtrack.com/rt-archive/more-cars-than-drivers-in-us)

[33] *Church Business Magazine*, March 2000

[34] Matthew 9:13, Hosea 6:6, Micah 6:8, Proverbs 21:32

[35] Luke 10:1-12

[36] Mark 8:36

[37] John 14:11

[38] Mark 1:38-39

[39] Acts 3:1-10, Acts 4:22

[40] Mark 8:36, Luke 10:1-20

[41] 1 Peter 2:12

[42] John 14:6

[43] Romans 5:8-10

[44] Mancini, Will, *Church Unique*, Jossey-Bass, 2008

Made in the USA
San Bernardino, CA
18 September 2014